Revolution of the Soul

by Richard Cole

www.amaricommunications.com

Revolution of the Soul

©2004, 2018 by Amari Communications
Published by Amari Enterprises
All Rights Reserved
ISBN: 978-0-557-52758-8

Revolution of the Soul

Table of Contents

Introduction   5

Soul Mate   6

Silence 2 Loud 2 Hear   10

Peace Beyond Fashion   12

Deeper   15

Absence   18

Intoxication   21

Passion (thefeelingwhenuknowwhyyouarehere)   23

Storms   25

Between Violence and Tranquility   27

Maat (In Dream)   31

Sunrise   34

From a Circle   36

Changes   39

Escape   41

What You Don't See   43

Destruction of Myth 46

April's Somebody 49

Ausar & Auset 51

Introduction

As an artist, it is a responsibility to pay a price. We express it so you don't have to. Joy, pain, love, hate. Protesting the conditions you live in or the conditions you work in. Having an artistic ability has allowed me to express myself in ways I have been either too shy or to introverted to shout out. I have been blessed to have various ways to express. Music, drawing, poetry, photography and storytelling have been the mediums in which most of you in the past and now many more, who are experiencing me for the first time in this book have come to know my thoughts or feelings.

This book isn't an autobiography, but it is an expression and commentary in poetic funk form of who I am and a part of the journey so far.

William Richard Cole, Jr
(Kofi Amari Roho Amen)

Soul Mate

Lover. Best Friend....Written in late 2000. This was written more about the search for a soul mate. Not about any one woman in mind, but the ideal and the possibilities of what she would represent.

Lover.

Every encounter in life adds up to you.

Shaped by mind's eye.

Freedom of soul.

Sister.

Tell me it's alright because only you know.

The one I talk to.

To remind me why I do what I need to go thru.

Sharing the journey & experience.

Learning thru relationships so complex.

Uncontrolled rhythms.

Balance of night & day.

Communication thru non linear understanding.

We communicate in our dreams.

The illusion of real life painted symbols as those near and far to me.

To point the way to becoming so that I can share the way with you.

I awoke to put my past to bed.

I live to be free instead.

To be me without apology.

You arrived like the sunrise.

You sing to me a beautiful surprise.

My friend.

With you I simply want to be.

My soul is the steady flow where body & mind in the center becomes the know.

Balance.

The rhythm of our existence to the beat of our growth.

The freedom of choice.

The words spoken from the voice.

In your absence there's emptiness.

I still feel your presence.

I've tasted the fruit of knowledge and I am no longer ashamed.

So forgive me dear friends if things aren't the same.

No judgment.

No placing blame.

I know my purpose.

I know where this river flows.

For my place on earth I dedicate my soul.

Everything I do for you I do for myself.

Unconditional.

Soul Mate.

Love so deep.

My spirit wants to fly.

One step closer to you.

I want to journey thru lifetimes and be swept away.

With the beauty of your smile to carry me each day.

Soul Mate.

Lover.

Sister.

My Friend.

Compelled to find the truth.

The other half of the sky.

You are my universe complete.

Silence 2 Loud 2 Hear

As time continues to unfold, there is a never ending need to lend a voice. Silence is often mistaken as indifference.

Is it to late to lend my voice?

Has my moment passed to have made a choice?

Has my mind journeyed into the universe only to be left adrift into empty verse?

Words that were never said.

Thoughts that never left my head.

Notes that were never played.

Love that was never made.

Or is my silence 2 loud 2 hear?

The dream is over.

I can still make it real.

My pain is deep.

I know I can feel.

This doesn't have to be an ending.

We can reach the end of the beginning.

Love is not a four letter word.

To love. To be Black. To be at peace.

Can you hear me or is there too much friction?

To love. To be proud. To stand.

Is there joy in this kind of repetition?

Or is my silence 2 loud 2 hear?

Peace Beyond Fashion

I thought this was pretty clever for the mid 1990's. Especially the 21ˢᵗ Century and it ain't gon' stop line which is used in my song Listen 2 The Band from The Reset EP. I'm still a funk revolutionary.

This is the real.

When it hits the top.

You can bet it goes pop.

21st Century and it ain't gon' stop.

Who wants to take it to the next step?

When was the revolution when I was the last one left?

Nu-Millennium genocide.

Some of us died a long time ago to teach us something simple.

Time as an illusion is running out.

A thousand years and most of us are still in doubt.

I believe there's hope.

I believe we can cope.

Revolution of the soul.

Take it to the mind.

Teach everyone how to funk in time.

Peace.

And it's said with passion.

You must dig....It is not a fashion.

Someday we can stop being tired and weary.

Someday the words I love you won't sound so eerie.

The chains we wear are in our minds.

There are no slaves on earth, but the concept still exists.

The excuses are several.

Some of them federal.

High Tech.

Institutionalized.

Generations wrecked.

Ain't it funky?

No, it's just fucked up.

Empty your cup, check your mind.

Check the rhythm in your own rhyme.

Peace.

And it's said with passion.

You must dig....It is not a fashion.

Much talk about keeping it real.

Talkin' loud and sayin' nothin.

No real concept of how you feel.

You may not want my opinion, but you're keepin' it real old.

Talk to me about the real after you've gained the world and lost
your soul.
Is it easier to live in video ghetto fantasies?

Will these words frighten you back into reality?

Ain't no fame gonna fall from the sky.

The search is within if you want to know why.

I've witnessed the strength of street knowledge.

Now give me a solution.

I can't stand to see another locked in another institution.

I want to see us one nation under a groove.

Instead of six feet underground.

Gettin'capped just for the funk of it.

Peace.

And it's said with passion.

U must dig....It is not a fashion.

Deeper

One of my favorite pieces. Pure poetry. It can be very romantic and it's very tantric lyrically. Sexiness is often that first hello.

Let me unlock your mind.

Take you on a journey beyond space and time.

To be set off on the first hello.

Now the invitation is on.

I want to explore the depths of your soul.

Physical isn't where it's at.

Though it plays a part.

And time is the only weapon I need 2 win your heart.

Insecurity an apprehension keeps us in a mellow state of contention.

Sometimes roller coasters can be fun.

Can I release your mind and be deep?

Don't stop before I begin.

In the beginning there is just a friend.

So these words aren't meant to undress you.

I want to know if my mind can caress you.

Maybe we met last lifetime.

Maybe we'll be deeper in the next.

Maybe this experience is the one that says it best.

To give a love never felt before.

If you don't want to go.

Then these words you can forever ignore.

Deeper.

A smile is orgasm in another form.

Deeper.

Having a hand to hold.

Or a feeling just as warm.

Deeper.

Like the joy in a child's first steps.

Deeper.

Wiping away your tears whenever you wept.

Deeper.

When your heart is in ascension.

Deeper.

Is the anticipation.

If my life was measured by just one day.

Then your love was the blink that changed it for a better way.

Exploration into the complexities of emotion.

Love has as many complexities as life itself.

The key is in the softness of a voice.

The truth inside as real as stars in the sky.

Feeling the universe from the first touch of your kiss.

The one moment we were apart.

Deeper was knowing it was you I missed.

Ask me how I want to spend eternity?

Deeper is wanting to spend it being the breath you take from one minute to the next.

Absence

***That conversation you have with in yourself when you let one or
'the one' get away.***

Experiences in life I mistook for just moments.

You don't know what you've got till it's gone.

Missing pieces to the puzzle to my life.

Living for the creation of song.

Living for the deepness of spiritual connection.

Living for the voice that says it's alright.

Should I continue this war with myself?

Should I go on without answers to the questions why?

Should I continue to get down with my bad self?

Should I go on with the truth and let the illusion die?

Second chances.

Are they worth it?

Am I the one who really deserves it?

Or is the truth something that I'm denied?

In this journey its only absence I find.

This morning I found a picture.

An image that once defined me.

A moment forever framed in history.

A time when there was no mystery.

A time when there was no absence of angels.

Artists pay the price so you don't have to.

The adventure decided if I should live or die.

Live for the moment.

Live for today.

Live for the ultimate high.

Live for just the funk of it.

Live for love.

Cause in this journey its only absence I find.

Never understood.

Why I go through the things I go through.

Get close to someone just to have them slip thru the sands of time.

What purpose do I fit in the grand design?

If this is right here.

Then where do I need to be?

Cause in this journey its only absence I find.

Yesterday when you left me.

Tomorrow I still had hope in.

Life went on without you by my side.

But trying to restructure the definition only widens my sorrow.

Living up to the reputation of my past is the penance for my crime.

I could hide behind the myth.

Like I know how to do.

It's only the truth I could never fool.

Flying without a net.

Dance underwater and not get wet.

At the final curtain.

It's still uncertain.

Whether to keep the act going all the time.

Cause in this journey its only absence I find.

Intoxication

*Total sexual intent. Romantic lust as it was said in the 80's.
Another one of my favorite romantic pieces.*

The taste of her lips.

Sweet wetness wine.

I drink to drown me.

I can't keep her off of my mind.

At first sight.

My spirit becomes a vessel of lust.

All awareness leaves at her touch.

Once I'm in her system.

This is the moment I start to live.

To her every wish.

To her every desire.

Everything for her happiness I want to give.

Intoxication.

A beautiful and dangerous thing.

Dangerous that you want to forsake everything.

Beautiful in that total devotion you want to bring.

Every thought replaces sleep.

To her existence forever my love is deep.

Every drop of her leaves me wanting more.
I don't need another confession.

She is the truth I've been living for.

My senses taken higher.

Totally blinded by desire.

Want and need.

Orgasmic indulgence in the pleasure of watching me bleed.

Intoxication.

Living for a high I don't regret when I come down.

Sweet forbidden pleasure that dances only for me.

Sweet poison.

My every breath for her insatiable taste.

I just can't leave her alone.

Passion (thefeelingwhenuknowwhyyouarehere)

Written at a time when there was doubt in my commitment as an artist. Remembering the days living in the Bay Area. It was a time of pure creativity and discovery.

Your mood is like spring.

Intoxicated by the day and a warm breeze.

And all I do is dream about you.

The scent of morning rain and music.

Longing to be with you.

Morning sun to wash away the darkness.

Midnight's passion mixed with sunrise intimacy.

Take a mood that's blue.

Paint it in chords striking and dark.

Even then you always end the day looking forward to tomorrow.

Whenever I'm with you, I'm captured by your rhythms.

Tempo slow as making love should be.

Tempo hittin' like passion ought to be.

Do we have to hurry?

Or will we be late if we don't?

Fast or slow.

With you it's always the right flow.

Can I slow down the day to experience you longer?

Can I fast forward to the part that sparks my heart?
Can I be alone with you after being with you all day?

Sunrise is the warmth of your smile.

Blue sky is the music of your beauty.

Morning is the color of your sexuality.

Spending my life with you is the magnetic of your personality.

Sunset is the song of your affection.

Your love is the prelude to summer.

Your essence is the dawn of my passion for you.

And I know where I need to be.

Storms

What happens when love steers you from your divine purpose. Of course it isn't love or the love is grossly one-sided. Its that baptism of fire that you must rise above and become what you are destined to be. God never makes storms that last.

I remember the ocean.

Like the memory of an old friend.

I remember the sunshine.

Because it reflected the life I once lived.

....the ocean was like an old friend.

She was the overcast to my day that was filled with joy.

Like the setting sun.

The dark blue to gray blanket.

That insured my sunny day would be done.

Illusions of nightfall.

A misled comfort.

She felt like a tropical breeze every time we made love.

Her wetness felt like drops of rain from heavens above.

There was calm.

Though our bodies moved like thunder.

My last thought was of the ocean.

While she became the hurricane that tore me asunder.

Her eyes were the lightning that shocked my heart.

Her words were the hail tore my dreams apart.
Every orgasm became my downfall.

Every beat of my heart was for a love that never existed at all.

She was the storm that washed all that I was away.

Though this storm has blown.

Dark clouds still haunt my sunny days.

With a chance of precipitation.

Weathering storms clearly define my role.

The quest for sunny days.

Is the quest to find peace for my soul.

....To embrace the ocean like an old friend.

Between Violence and Tranquility

Inspired by a work of fiction in which the character was between violence and tranquility or violence and something yet to be decided. It inspired my journey into zen. Always balancing the equation.

Darkness is another friend.

No Lights.

Blinds drawn.

Darkness feels like a blanket.

Comfort from all the injustice that exist.

It's not just my pain.

Sometimes it's the pain I feel for others.

It makes me want to fight back.

I can fly.

Sometimes I realize I don't have wings.

Sometimes knights fall.

Voices in my mind speak confusion.

What am I?

What I am.

Some are.

Others become.

Become.

Can't stay.

Can't let go.
I fight because I'm attacked.

I'm judged.

I'm afraid.

To be strong was only an appearance.

A mask.

The image that kept everyone else outside.

A lie.

Revenge not for being born.

Revenge for the torture once I got here.

Can I forgive and move on?

Can I lash out at everything and everyone except the truth?

Will I destroy the truth or will I destroy the myth?

The myth of all image, insecurity and funk.

The truth that I am somebody.

Divided soul.

Each piece auctioned to serve selfish needs.

Spirit beaten until it begged to be taken away.

Say you want a revolution?

Wait till I tell you about the one for my soul.

The future becomes a curtain closed.

Because I could no longer live up to my past.

Broken.

I love you.

There's nothing I can learn or want.

I love you.

I've caused so much pain.

I never meant to hurt.

I'm asking for forgiveness.

I forgive you too.

Forgiveness is song performed by peace.

Love.

Unconditional love.

Love me.

I don't want to live in darkness.

I only need darkness for light.

Balance.

The color will show.

If you listen to its color.

I just want to go on a different trip.

I just want to grow.

I create because it's a gift from God.

To seek a better path for my soul.

Love.

And just a little understanding.

Peace is what I desire.

What no myth can achieve.

Between violence and tranquility.

Between violence and something yet to be decided.

Choose.

Maat (In Dream)

*Based on a dream I had summer of 1994. It was the beginning of
sequence of dreams that inspired the title of this book and other
poems in this book as well as a few songs that may see the light
of day. Always balancing the equation.*

I took this journey.

I took a walk in a rain forest.

My spirit didn't realize it was dream.

In this garden.

I was in conflict.

With purpose.

With destiny.

With attachments that bind me like grapes on a vine.

I was captivated by this beauty.

Heaven would only be a cliché'.

Let's just say this is paradise.

Before I realized this was a metaphor.

I was thirsty.

I came by a fountain that was near a waterfall.

I drank.

I drank.

And it seemed everything I did.

Couldn't ease the thirst (The questions that were hidden).

As I indulge in this insatiable lust.
My soul became disturbed by the thirst.

Sound liquefied from the spring.

Spiritual wild.

Communication in song.

Liquid sound took form of a beautiful soul.

I saw music become an angel.

Beauty beyond this plane of reality.

She whispered my name.

With voices suspended in perfection.

Each syllable of my name held by angels in one body.

Her essence bathed me in calm.

I experienced life for the first time when she spoke to me.

Water alone will not quench you; your thirst is greater than your thirst for water.

She held my face in her hands.

Beyond the confines of time.

In under a second.

I was aware of the universe.

I understood it.

Or was it my own soul I was beginning to understand?

What she unlocked was the truth.
The tranquility I had been seeking.

I wanted to ask her so many questions.

About myself.

About life.

About the paths we take.

About our power to choose.

About the mysteries locked inside my mind.

Her only reply as she faded away....

Don't worry, It's alright.

Then I woke to find myself on this journey.

Sunrise

Optimisim in poetry.

This is where the journey begins.

Wisdom gathered by experience.

Everything I create brings me closer to my destination.

Baptized in this with the rays of the summer sun.

Nothing else gives me the feeling of flight.

Time means nothing.

It flows through me.

The soul considered the one whispers inspiration.

Harmony echoes from her soul.

Peaceful and wild.

Sunrise.

Salvation is its real name.

My soul touches harmony in a symphony.

The universe is the maestro.

Moving in rhythm to its balanced equation.

I gather the fruit of my creativity.

I net it into an armor uncontested.

To protect a heart that beats with renewed conviction.

Sunrise.
Resurrection.

The phoenix has flown.

Let the funk flow.

From a Circle

Maybe sub-consciously the title is Ancient Egyptian philosophy, but I was really inspired by the rhythm of The Beatles song 'Dig A Pony' and was trying to write something in that vein.

I dug myself from a circle.

No more round and round.

Nothing comes to dreamers and so on.

Where there was silence.

There is sound.

Maybe now you can feel your own pain.

If you really want to.

Maybe now you can rise above what you are.

Deeper than what you are.

You can choose one path when your spirit calls.

God has placed them all.

So what you are is not etched in stone.

Just when you choose based on what is known.

I picked a nu style.

High fashion dazed in a paisley funk.

So I could put a chaotic beat to everything I know.

Put a little funk to everything you know.

For too long I've tried to run.

From the one place I cannot hide.
Now its time to break the chains that bind.

To free the soul that's trapped inside.

Time.

She knows to keep on moving.

Flowing thru all in life.

Trust in the moment to provide.

Time.

Disillusion of all illusion.

Truth is all we'll find.

To become enlightened is to become.

In a fraction the fabric of the future is undone.

Time.

Shaped by magic tricks of the mind.

The past is reflected by the mood you're in.

The future depended on the optimistic and pessimistic war within.

I left a circle.

So I could leave you to sit on every idea you have.

So you could not realize every dream you have.

I formed an experience.

So I could listen to every color in my head.

Go just a little deeper instead.

The past has taught me nothing.

Just brought me thru another day.

Everything I've learned still can't find the meaning.

Just gives me another way.

All there is...

Truth.

Outside the circle everything is like you want it to.

Changes

Written around the summer of 1996 during a 2 week period of writing. My thoughts about adapting to change.

Into a memory here and now slips away.

Comfortable with today turning into yesterday.

So I remember everything as a fine morning.

Though some moments left without warning.

Love is a feeling that has stood the test of time.

As time always brings changes.

May changes bring a moment like this again.

Time in its fabric unfolds before me.

So many possibilities ahead.

Yesterday I clearly see.

A sunrise I will always cherish.

Though you're gone I know my day will never perish.

All things in time changes.

So I live in the here and now.

Feeling better about tomorrow.

What I know now prepares me for all of its joys and sorrows.

Good things to come.

They may not always last.

All things learned is what we make of our past.

While around us things always change.

Escape

Inspired by Prince and the whole symbol/Artist formerly known as period. I wanted to escape as well and be in a position to be the artist I want to be.

For too long I've tried to run.

From the one place I cannot hide.

Prisoner to chains that bind.

Longing to free the soul that's trapped inside.

My biggest fear consumed me.

A predator stalking me through time.

Why did I let it take control?

What was it that denied my true self?

Some days I don't even know.

For too long I've tried to run.

From the one place that I cannot hide.

Prisoner to haters that want to keep me blind.

Determined to keep my soul trapped inside.

Time.

She knows to keep moving.

Flowing through me.

Trust in the moment to provide.

Time.

Illusions.

Lies.

Fantasy.

For too long I've tried to run.

From the one place I cannot hide.

Now its time to break the chains that bind.

To free the soul trapped inside.

What You Don't See

Pure Sly Stone inspired funk. Music to be released at a later date.

I've played my funk for you.

Was I what you wanted me to be?

Was my love the rhythm you needed to funk to your own beat?

Did I make you high in all the right places?

Did I cry with all the right faces?

I've played my funk for you.

But you still can't compete.

Because of what you don't see.

There's no room for conformity.

It needs to fall.

There's no room for negativity.

We don't have to fight about it all.

I had to make a choice.

I had to not be afraid of the power of my own voice.

To be something else.

To be enlightened.

I want to go higher.

Empty my cup and take a sip.

Take this journey on another trip.

There's no emptiness in my city.

Just empty minded fools sittin' pretty.

How much longer before we can see?

How can we make this complete?

Life is very short.

End of the beginning could be a day away.

No excuses.

The problem isn't that deep.

It's what you don't see.

Talk to me.

We need communication.

Talk to me.

Let's look for balance.

Look beyond what you don't see.

I've bared my soul for you.

But you still won't put me on.

Can we live this moment together?

Will you appreciate me when I'm gone?

Nothing seen that isn't shown.

I still believe.

What's impossible?

It's what you don't see.

Destruction of Myth

Ego is an illusion.

What's the difference between the image you perceive and the one I allow you to see?

Nothing.

Both are non-existent.

To those who can and cannot understand.

The myth is not home anymore.

Maat said it's alright.

From inside my soul.

One door closed.

Another one opened.

I need to feel the funk inside my soul.

If I cannot be free.

Then I cannot be me.

The myth kept you from hurting the reality I cherished most.

The myth also hurt you more times than you cared to know.

To whom it may concern.

I've learned to let it go.

You couldn't look beyond what force was fed to you through time.

What you couldn't have in reality you tried to mold.

You were too blind.

The threat to my heart was too much.

The myth kept me safe and kept you real.

Protection from souls whose only aim is to destroy.

You got to understand.

Dreams are enslaved when you are not allowed to try.

Answers are no good without the questions why.

Let those who don't know worry about cash flow.

I need to tell the truth and satisfy my soul.

I am not what I am because I have to be.

Destruction of myth allowed me to be who I am because I choose to be.

In my mind there is peace.

Balance is all I believe in.

I don't need you to choreograph the definition of my existence.

I've served divorce papers on this game.

Love sings to my soul in love.

So that I may speak to you in real.

Destruction of myth.

The end of the illusion.

I'm living the color of my dream.

Find your own solution.

The myth is over.

End of the beginning.

April's Somebody

From age 12 to 14, I was literally in love with the month of April. I really must have been deeply in love with someone in a past life. Just something about being in my room, spring air thru the open window. Very spiritual and romantic. I think I must have wanted to meet or fall in love with that special girl in my imagination. Its also my favorite time of the year to listen to The Beatles' Revolver or Prince's Sign 'O' The Times.

Midnight rain turns into a liquid sunshine morning.

The world doesn't get painted like this much anymore.

April's moisture filled with every breath with love.

Songs of beauty poured from the souls of doves.

Only in love with the gift of life.

And the warmth of April's sunlight.

Pretty April morning.

Psychedelic daydream.

Sitar tinged melody woven into silk lined soul.

Waking meditation.

It moves and removes.

And you fall in love with love.

Take a trip outside.

Gaze at the angel with the overcast eyes.

Feel snug as the breeze caresses you as you walk.

Feel kissed by morning as the rain says goodbye.

Feel the joy in the pounding of your heart.

As rainbows puddles are placed at your feet.

The joy of being April's somebody.
Happiness sends you an angel.

To carry you on her wings through the day.

Sun or rain.

Joy or pain.

She carries you home.

Reflections are disguised as the beauty of the world around you.

Long for the love you have.

Long for the love you lost.

Long for the first hello and the moment you fall in love all over again.

The joy of being April's somebody.

Ausar & Auset

The last piece for this book. Written early 2001.

There was beginning.

There was light.

There was us.

There was life.

There was purpose.

You were my reason.

So out of love was conceived the universe.

To have you for eternity.

I give you time.

To illustrate your beauty.

I give you a garden called earth.

Inspired by you there is nature.

Fruits to quench your hunger or thirst.

May it fill you as your essence fills me.

To reflect everything of you inside.

The sun has permission to rise.

In memory of when your lips 1st touched mine.

The moon and stars harmonize with your soul.

Out of passion I blanket you with night.

As creation tastes what was forbidden or what was meant to learn.

Infinite knowledge now secrets long hidden.

In effect, I died for you.

To find the way back through darkness.

My desire to remain beside you.

The rain is the arousal of your passion.

Storms are your orgasm.

I am humbled because you are my balance.

Guilty because sometimes I give you a world so cold.

I go to war for your honor as well as my soul.

There are no mistakes in life only lessons.

Heaven exists as the eternal reminder of your smile.

A choice to remain.

Or reincarnate to win your love again.